Putting a Stop to Wildfires

by Erin Cameron

Scott Foresman
is an imprint of

PEARSON

Glenview, Illinois • Boston, Massachusetts • Chandler, Arizona
Upper Saddle River, New Jersey

Photographs
Every effort has been made to secure permission and provide appropriate credit for photographic material. The publisher deeply regrets any omission and pledges to correct errors called to its attention in subsequent editions.

Unless otherwise acknowledged, all photographs are the property of Pearson.

Photo locations denoted as follows: Top (T), Center (C), Bottom (B), Left (L), Right (R), Background (Bkgd)

CVR © SuperStock, Inc./SuperStock; **3** © Falk Kienas/Shutterstock; **4** © Reuters/Corbis; **5** Getty Images; **6** © SuperStock, Inc./SuperStock; **7** © Gene Blevins/LA Daily News/ Corbis; **8** Mike McMillan/Spotfire Images; **9** © Bettmann/Corbis; **11** (TL) © Photo Network/Alamy Images, (TR) © Hot Ideas/Index Open, (CR) © Greg Wright/Alamy Images, (BR) © Hot Ideas/Index Open, (BL) Getty Images; **12** © Image Source ; **13** Corbis; **14** Mike McMillan/Spotfire Images; **15** © Reuters/Corbis; **16** AP Images; **17** © Kevin R. Morris/Corbis; **18** AP Images; **19** Getty Images.

ISBN 13: 978-0-328-51673-5
ISBN 10:   0-328-51673-2

4 5 6 7 8 9 10 V0FL 15 14 13 12 11

A storm builds over the Rocky Mountains in Colorado.

Southern Colorado is a beautiful place, but the weather can change quickly. On a Thursday afternoon in July 2005, gray clouds gathered in the sky. The **wind** picked up, bending trees and snapping flags. Lightning cracked over the mountains, followed by booming thunder.

People living in this part of Colorado eyed the storm and worried. A dry, sunny summer had cooked the earth to a hard crust. Grasses and trees were as dry and as yellow as old newspaper. One lightning strike could start a fire. With the wind blowing the way it was, a wildfire would spread quickly.

Wind Pushes the Fires On

People were right to worry. Before morning, lightning had struck more than a dozen times. Fires dotted the mountainsides, ate up flatlands, and raged through canyons.

Hard-blowing winds would feed the flames for the next several days. Fires would tear across the land, racing southward.

To make matters worse, some of the fires burned near Mesa Verde National Park. This parkland was once the home of the Pueblo people.

Lightning can spark wildfires.

Native American Pueblo buildings on the cliffs of Mesa Verde are 700 to 800 years old. It would be terrible if the ancient villages burned in a fire.

Firefighters jumped onto trucks and into airplanes. Bulldozers roared into action, digging up long stretches of soil in front of the fires. If firefighters could dig up everything that might burn, they might be able to keep the fire from spreading.

Pueblo people lived in these cliff dwellings more than 700 years ago.

Fighting to Gain Control

In places where bulldozers could not reach, crews of highly trained firefighters called "hotshots" rushed to control the flames. Like the bulldozers, the hotshot crews dug fire lines of soil to stop the fires from spreading.

Tanker airplanes and helicopters dumped water and flame retardant on areas near the fire. This **method** of fighting the fire was meant to help keep fires from spreading, but the wind that day drove the flames on.

Eight more highly trained firefighters called "smokejumpers" arrived. They scrambled into planes, **concentrating** on fires in out-of-the-way places. Only two of these smokejumpers were able to jump, because the fires were just too dangerous. The firefighters on the ground requested more men and women to come and help. It was a bad situation.

Firefighters try to control the flames from the air.

Hotshot crews fight wildfires on the ground.

Hotshots

A wildfire is one that burns across broad areas of wilderness. The men and women who fight wildfires use many different methods. Some fly over fires and use special tools to learn exactly which areas of a wilderness are burning. Others drive trucks or large firefighting equipment.

Hotshots fight wildfires on the ground. Their specialty is working up close on big, dangerous fires.

Hotshots and smokejumpers travel all over the country to fight wildfires during the fire season, which lasts from May to October. They may be called to remote areas in places such as Alaska, California, or Florida, where wildfires can spread quickly during the warm, dry summer months.

Hotshots usually work in crews of about twenty men and women. They are "on call" during fire season, ready to go wherever wildfires are burning. Sometimes they travel in trucks or helicopters. Other times, they must walk to the fire.

Once there, hotshots clear out trees and **underbrush** that burn quickly. They dig up grass and stumps to make a fire line, a broad band of bare soil. In some cases, they even start backfires. This means that they set a new fire to burn toward one that is already burning. If all goes as planned, the two fires join up and burn themselves out.

Hotshots dig a fire line.

Hotshots at rest

During fire season, hotshot crews spend weeks at a time away from home. Their workday may be 16 or 18 hours long. They may need to sleep on the ground, if they get to sleep at all. Smoke, poison ivy, dust, and many other dangers are a regular part of the hotshots' working day.

Hotshots' Tools and Equipment

As you can tell, being a hotshot is hard, dangerous work. To help them stay safe on the job, hotshots wear special clothing. Even though fire sites are often very warm, hotshots wear heavy jackets made from materials that don't burn easily. These jackets are usually bright yellow, and they have broad stripes that catch and reflect light. Firefighters want to be able to see each other, even in dark smoke or at night. They wear helmets with flaps that can cover their faces. These helmets protect their heads from falling tree branches. Heavy gloves protect their hands from burns, and boots cover their feet.

Since they often work in places where there are no roads, hotshots sometimes carry everything they need. This includes drinking water and heavy tools. It may also include a chain saw or small water pump. A hotshot's backpack might also hold a fire shelter, flashlight, first aid kit, food, and map. Along with these items, hotshots carry all the usual firefighters' gear in their backpacks, such as a radio, axe, and shovel.

jacket

helmet

gloves

axe

boots

Training Is Important

Fighting wildfires is backbreaking work, so these men and women stay in very good shape. Part of their training includes walking long trails while they carry heavy packs. Before the season starts, hotshots must pass tests to show that they are strong enough to do the job. Their strength and **dedication** will save lives.

There's more to hotshot training than being fit. Hotshots must understand how fires behave and be able to predict what the flames will do next. If a fire becomes too dangerous, hotshots must know how to keep themselves and others safe. They must know how to use all firefighting tools, from axes to water pumps. Since helicopters sometimes carry hotshots into and out of fires, they must also know how to work safely around aircraft.

Smokejumpers jump from cargo planes like this to fight wildfires.

Smokejumpers

Some of the fires that raced across Colorado in 2005 were in heavy forest on rough land. The flames were far from roads and were very hard to reach. In this type of wildfire, it's **essential** to call in a special breed of firefighter known as a smokejumper.

A smokejumper flies into a burning area in a cargo plane and jumps out, wearing a **parachute**.

Wind is sometimes a problem. It can blow parachutes in the wrong direction. So, before anyone jumps, a spotter drops streamers from the airplane and watches to see where the streamers land.

If the streamers reach the ground in a safe landing zone, then smokejumpers jump the next time the plane circles around. If the streamers blow into an unsafe landing zone, then the airplane circles a second time, and the spotter looks for a safer landing zone. Sometimes smokejumpers must jump out above the fire and let the wind carry them to a safer place. Being a smokejumper is truly dangerous work.

A smokejumper on his way to work

Supplies are dropped from the cargo plane after the smokejumpers have landed.

After dropping smokejumpers, the airplane circles around again. This time it drops supplies and tools that the smokejumpers will need for fighting the fire. Smokejumpers sometimes work near the fire for a few days at a time. When the airplane drops supplies, it also drops sleeping bags and enough food and water for two days.

Smokejumpers fight wildfires in the same ways hotshots do. They clear brush and trees and dig out fire lines. Their main job is to control the blaze by removing its fuel—trees, brush, and dry grass.

Throughout the fire season, smokejumpers travel to wherever they are needed, just like hotshots. Every year their job takes them far from home for long periods of time.

What Clothing Do Smokejumpers Wear?

The clothing of a smokejumper is specially made for jumping out of airplanes. All smokejumpers wear a harness connected to a parachute. They wear jumpsuits that are padded to protect them when they hit the ground. The jumpsuits are made from material that doesn't burn easily. The collar on a smokejumper's suit stands up to cover and protect the neck as he or she slips through treetops. Smokejumpers wear helmets with face protection, much like those that football players wear. Like hotshots, they protect their feet with boots.

high collar

harness

helmet with face protection

jumpsuit

boots

Smokejumper Training

Smokejumper training is a bit different from hotshot training, but it is just as necessary. Smokejumpers learn to jump safely and to **steer** themselves while they fall through the air. If they get hung up in a tree, they must know how to drop safely to the ground. If they land on hard ground, they must know how to roll to avoid getting hurt. They exercise often and stay in tiptop physical condition.

Like hotshots, smokejumpers are specially trained to understand fires. They know what will happen if the wind changes direction, or if a fire leaps over a fire line. They know what to do in an emergency, when a fire becomes too dangerous.

Five Days after the First Lightning Strike

In southern Colorado in 2005, high winds continued to blow. Five days after the first lightning strike, firefighters finally had the flames under control. Tired and dirty, they could at last catch their breath.

Thousands of acres of land had burned. But experts had shown firefighters where the ancient Pueblo buildings stood. This helped the crews save the historic Pueblo villages at Mesa Verde National Park.

Wildfires scarred the Colorado landscape in 2005.

Even though the fires were under control, there was still a lot of work to be done. Flames had to be put out, and the area had to be made safe. These last stages of firefighting are called "mopping up," and local firefighters sometimes take over this job.

Outside of fire season, hotshots and smokejumpers do other kinds of work. They work on parks and trails, and they train for the next season. They work throughout the year to maintain and protect the country's parks and forests.

These firefighters' experience, leadership, and bravery help keep the rest of us safe from dangerous wildfires.

Smokejumpers are airlifted out of the remote wooded areas.

Glossary

concentrating *v.* paying close attention; focusing the mind

dedication *n.* the act of setting apart for a purpose

essential *adj.* absolutely necessary; very important

method *n.* way of doing something

parachute *n.* a device shaped like an umbrella, made of nylon or silk, that allows people or objects to fall slowly after dropping out of an aircraft

steer *v.* to guide the course of

underbrush *n.* bushes and small trees growing under large trees in woods or forests; undergrowth.

wind *n.* air in motion